What Children Play

by Robin Raymer

Harcourt

Orlando   Boston   Dallas   Chicago   San Diego

Visit **The Learning Site!**

www.harcourtschool.com

What do you like to play with?
Many children play with dolls, cars,
planes, and cranes. They use
computers to play games. They also
play games with spinners and cards
that give directions.

Some of the toys you play with may use batteries. The toys buzz, talk, walk, jump, and twitch.

Today most children don't worry about finding time to play. Long ago, it was different.

Long ago, children had to help
their families. There was a lot of
work to do in the house and outside.
Children did not have a lot of time to
play.

Most people made their own toys. They made them with things that were right at home.

Toy makers might make toys from wood, metal, paper, or rubber. The toys were made by machine.

Rolling, Riding, and Rocking

Some people liked to skate on ice. There is no ice in summer, so in 1860 Mr. James Plimpton made a new kind of skate with wheels. People could skate all year long.

You had to be tall to
ride a bike like this!

Here is a horse
on wheels.

Does this
look like a
sled you
might use?

Many Kinds of Dolls

Native Americans made many dolls. They used corn, grass, and deerskin. The dolls were decorated with shells, beads, or feathers.

Only rich people had fancy dolls like this. If you wanted to hold this doll, you'd have to promise not to drop her. That's because her head might break.

People who could not buy dolls made them with things at home.

People made rag dolls from leftover cloth. Rag dolls may have had button eyes and yarn hair.

Some girls played with paper dolls. They took good care of them so they would last a long time.

This dollhouse is filled with tiny things. Long ago, children and grown-ups made all of the things for a dollhouse on their own.

The first plastic dolls looked like this. The plastic was very hard. Today plastic dolls are much softer.

From Horses to Cars to Planes

Toys show us what life was like long ago.

In the early 1900s, toy makers started to make toy cars.

Joshua L. Cowen made the first toy electric trains. He called them Lionel trains. Lionel was his middle name!

Toys like this showed children how workers did their jobs.

Children played with toy planes. Long ago, not many people flew in airplanes.

Toy Animals

This toy monkey is made from a sock.

Teddy bears became popular about a hundred years ago.

Blocks and More Blocks

These ABC blocks were called spelling blocks.

Even before blocks were made, children used pieces of wood or rocks to build things. Wooden blocks were easy to make and children still love them.

Penny Banks

Toy banks like these made saving money a lot of fun. Parts moved as a penny went into the bank.

A long time ago, you could buy a lot with a penny!